STAR WARS

R2-D2

STAR WARS®

R2-D2

AN INSIDE LOOK AT THE ULTIMATE ASTROMECH DROID

WRITTEN BY MICHAEL KOGGE

INCREDI BUILDS™

A Division of Insight Editions, LP
San Rafael, California

INTRODUCTION

The diminutive astromech droid known as R2-D2 may not look like much, but he's one of the toughest, most versatile droids ever to roll on three legs. He can pilot starships, carry out complicated repairs, record messages, and even play holochess. Over his long and storied career, R2 has managed to avoid system resets to develop a quirky personality and an independent mindset. This can make him a frustrating coworker yet the most endearing of companions.

Some engineers say a sense of humor can never be programmed, but that has never stopped R2-D2 from developing one. While his counterpart C-3PO believes suffering to be their lot in life, R2-D2 seems quite content to chirp merrily (or rudely) at whatever challenges the galaxy throws at him. His devil-may-care attitude often gets him into trouble but at the same time gives him the key to getting out of it. Experience has trained his logic circuits that the quickest route out of a jam is to compute new and seemingly illogical ways of employing his equipment. R2-D2 has learned that his gadgets best serve him in situations that don't match their manufacturers' specifications.

R2-D2's role in galactic events may have inflated his digital ego—at least according to C-3PO—but it has not changed his devotion to his comrades. It's rare to find a droid as loyal and reliable as R2-D2, even if he can be persnickety and stubborn at times. Numerous upgrades over the years keep R2 humming along with the latest models while other units of his age have been resigned to the trash compactor. As long as his friends still need him, R2-D2 will always have the pluck and resourcefulness to keep rolling on and never become obsolete.

BASIC CAPABILITIES

Primarily engineered for astronavigational assistance and starship maintenance, R2-D2 also doubles as a general-purpose utility droid. His functionality extends to holographic recording, image projection, data storage, fire extinguishing, and sensor scanning. He's even been known to serve drinks, proving he fits his manufacturer's famous advertising slogan: "No job is over this little guy's head."

TECHNICAL SPECIFICATIONS

MANUFACTURER: Industrial Automation

MODEL: R2 series

DROID CLASS: Two

HEIGHT: 1.09 m (3 ft, 6 in)

COST: 5,000 Imperial credits for starter model

COMMUNICATION MODULE: Binary (droidspeak)

GENDER MODULE: Male

TRIPODAL DESIGN

Three hydraulic legs permit a sturdy, upright position on a variety of surfaces for all-terrain maneuverability. Two of the legs are always operational, while the middle leg can be extended for extra stability or retracted for speed.

RADAR EYE: Photoreceptor can monitor and measure the visible, infrared, and electromagnetic spectra

PROCESSOR STATE INDICATOR: Displays performance of internal systems

MOTORIZED ROLLER TREAD: Mobility controlled by powerbus cables

MAGNETIC LOCK: For firm attachment to starship hulls

POWER CELLS: Can energize movement, even if body or brain is disabled

HOLOCAM ACCESSORIES

The astromech can capture and show moments in time, making him an ideal messenger.

ROTATING PROJECTOR: Can be aimed to display holographic messages and broadcasts in sizes suited to the surrounding environment and audience

CAMERA: Radar eye records full three-dimensional figures.

PERISCOPE SYSTEM: R2-D2 has multiple antennae that provide visual and biochemical data.

AUDITORY MICROPHONES: Distinguish important sounds from a range of environmental noise

SENSORY INPUT

R2-D2's full-service sensor package includes a number of features.

ELECTROMAGNETIC SENSOR UNIT: Measures surrounding electromagnetic spectrum

DROID OF ALL TRADES

R2-D2 is not your ordinary, off-the-rack astromech. Over his many years in operation, R2 has acquired an array of assorted gadgetry that would seem ill-serving for a droid of his class. Yet all of these instruments have come in handy at one point or another—and are often used in a manner their designers never dreamed!

PERISCOPE (ENVIRONMENTAL SCANNER): Detects life-forms and examines air content through basic chemical analysis

MISCELLANEOUS TOOLS

R2-D2 hosts many other features that few know about until he calls them into action.

PERISCOPE (VISUAL DATA): Extendable above dome for a 360-degree view and sweep of surroundings, with signal booster

ELECTRIC PROD: When R2 requires a zap to get things going, this packs quite a charge.

DATA CARD READER: Accepts a degree of shapes, sizes, and formats, from data-tapes to holodiscs

UNIVERSAL EXTENDER ARM: Can be fitted with a wide array of tips, from computer interface prongs to saws and manipulators of various sizes.

COMPUTER INTERFACE: One of R2's most used implements is his computer interface tool, which plugs into dataports for exchanging information.

EMITTER NOZZLE Located under hinged dome panel; sprays either fire extinguishing foam vent fumes to creat a smoke screen

ATTITUDE JETS: Propel R2-D2 through space and atmospheres

GRIPPER: Pincers give R2-D2 the ability to grab and manipulate exterior objects.

ARMS

A carousel of internal rotating appendages extends from R2-D2's dome and cylindrical body. Various fittings like welding tips, cutting saws, and even beverage dispensers can expand an arm's utility for almost any purpose.

FEARLESS FLYER

Despite possessing three legs, R2-D2 was designed for duties off the ground. He's at home in the rear socket of a starfighter, has no qualms making extravehicular repairs in space, and can even fly all on his own when needed.

COURAGEOUS COPILOT

Any account of the legendary piloting of Luke Skywalker and his father Anakin would be incomplete without mention of their astromech droid. Though Jedi reflexes give Luke and Anakin an incredible advantage in space battles, they would be lost if not for R2-D2's invaluable assistance. While they do the breakneck flying, R2 crunches the numbers. His duties are numerous and require true versatility.

SYSTEMS STATUS: In conjunction with a starship's computers, R2 maintains a vigilant watch on the functionality of all components, including weapons, in order to carry out immediate repairs or boost power to different systems.

BATTLE ANALYSIS: Studyir space engagement from multi angles and data sources, R2 estimates best-case scenario provides telemetry and guidar to the pilots.

HYPERSPACE HELPER: Astromech droids store a number of preprogrammed hyperspace jumps for emergency exits but can also connect with the onboard navcomputer to calculate new vectors into lightspeed.

SECOND PILOT: If Luke or Anakin are ever incapacitated or in deep hibernation sleep, they trust R2-D2 to run the show and fly their starfighter.

ROCKET RESCUE

Early in R2's career, he was equipped with swiveling attitude jets that popped out from the sides of his primary legs, allowing him to launch from a surface if necessary and propel himself a short distance in the atmosphere. R2 also used them to maneuver underwater and in zero-gravity conditions. A small canister of fuel was installed inside R2-D2's cylinder to power thrust for protracted flights. Later, these jets were swapped out from his chassis to make room for other features.

CANTANKEROUS COUNTERPARTS

Though R2-D2 and C-3PO are droids, they have somehow overridden their programming to become the greatest of friends. The evidence is in their behavior. They bicker and quarrel endlessly, often tramping or trundling away from each other in a huff. Their petty disputes can make them highly inefficient—sometimes to the point where their owners have threatened to fit them with restraining bolts. Yet whenever one of them is in danger, the other hazards his circuits to make sure that their companion is safe. Theirs is an unbreakable bond that survives even memory wipes.

PROUD PARTNERS

After Anakin Skywalker fell on the volcanic plains of Mustafar and Padmé Amidala lost her life, R2-D2 and C-3PO found themselves under the supervision of a single master, Senator Bail Organa. Thus began their official association as counterparts.

FIRST IMPRESSIONS

R2-D2 initially encountered a semi-assembled C-3PO in Anakin Skywalker's bedroom on Tatooine. His first beep to C-3PO caused the protocol droid some embarrassment as R2 announced that "his parts" were showing.

KEPT SECRETS

A recalcitrant R2-D2 left his golden friend in Tatooine's Dune Sea in order to embark on a secret mission he refused to explain. C-3PO eventually found R2 in a Jawa sandcrawler and vouched for the droid's usefulness to Luke Skywalker.

HEAD HAULER

When C-3PO's head got attached to a battle droid's body amid a fierce fight between Jedi and Separatists on Geonosis, R2-D2 wheeled into the fray, attached a cable to the protocol droid's head, and then wrenched it off and towed it to safety.

THE THINGS I DO FOR YOU

After C-3PO was blasted into spare parts on Cloud City and experienced the distress of Chewbacca's hasty reassembly, R2-D2 repaired the protocol droid to full functionality.

FRIENDLY SHOVE

R2-D2 gave a nervous C-3PO a forceful bump off Jabba's soon-to-blow sail barge, saving his counterpart from being caught in the explosion.

HERO OF THE REPUBLIC

R2-D2's feats of bravery during the waning years of the Republic demonstrate that courage is not a quality limited to flesh-and-blood heroes.

INVASION OF NABOO

R2-D2 distinguished himself while serving in Queen Amidala's retinue.

FOCUSED FIXER: While Trade Federation battleships blasted his astromech compatriots, R2-D2 stayed firm to the hull of the queen's Royal Starship and repaired the vessel's shield generator so it could escape through the planetary blockade of Naboo. The Queen later honored R2—a rare distinction for a droid.

BACKSOCKET 'BOT: R2-D2 assisted nine-year-old Anakin Skywalker in flying a Naboo N-1 starfighter and destroying the Trade Federation control ship. The feat deactivated the battle droids on Naboo's surface, ending the occupation.

REPUBLIC IN PERIL

When the Separatists threatened the galaxy, R2-D2 remained in the charge of Anakin Skywalker and joined the budding Jedi Knight on many perilous quests.

POLITICAL PATROL: After a failed assassination attempt on Padmé Amidala's life, R2-D2 watched over the senator in her bedchamber and accompanied Anakin in guarding her during their trip to Naboo.

SENATOR SAVIOR: R2-D2 fired his booster rockets to fly through the droid factory on Geonosis. Finding Padmé trapped inside an empty vat, R2-D2 deposited himself near a terminal port. He issued a command to halt the molten ore from being poured into the vat, then rotated the vat so Padmé could escape.

BUZZ BEATER:
During the starfighter battle over Coruscant, R2-D2—plugged into the socket of Anakin Skywalker's Jedi interceptor—fended off a buzz droid and fed the Jedi Knight accurate telemetry to help turn the tide of the conflict.

BATTLE BLAZER: In the hangar of General Grievous's dreadnought, R2-D2 showered two super battle droids with flammable lubricant, which he ignited with his booster jets. Once free, he carried out Anakin Skywalker's commands to operate the turbolift so his master could save Chancellor Palpatine.

HERO OF THE REBELLION

R2-D2 may not have been able to prevent the fall of the Republic, but he was instrumental in defeating the Galactic Empire.

DEATH STAR DROID

If not for R2-D2, the Rebel Alliance might have been helpless against the Empire's first Death Star.

TRASH TALKER: R2-D2 communicated with the Death Star's computers to shut down all garbage compactors on the detention levels, thereby saving his new master Luke Skywalker and his friends from being flattened.

MEMORY MODULE: Princess Leia Organa of Alderaan stored the technical readouts to the Death Star battle station inside the memory banks of R2-D2. She also commanded him to fulfill a top-secret mission on Tatooine: Find the desert hermit Obi-Wan Kenobi and deliver the Death Star plans to the Rebel Alliance.

IMPERIAL RETALIATION

Though obsolete compared to other models, R2-D2 continued to serve Luke Skywalker, even when the Empire was on the verge of vanquishing the Rebels for good.

DAGOBAH DRIFTER: R2-D2 journeyed with Luke to the mysterious Dagobah system, where he provided company for his master and watched over the swamped X-wing fighter.

CLOUD CREATOR: Cut off from his master on Cloud City, R2-D2 ran into C-3PO and his other friends while they were being pursued by stormtroopers. R2-D2 fired his fire extinguisher toward the troopers, producing a smoke screen so the rebels could get away.

REBIRTH OF THE JEDI

Never showing his age, R2-D2 witnessed the fall of the Jedi and the rise of a new hope for their ancient order.

DRINK DISPENSER: Jabba the Hutt's supervisor droid, EV-9D9, fitted the astromech unit for a task that was an insult to R2-D2's design: serving beverages for the scum and villainy on the crime lord's sail barge. Nonetheless, R2 used this opportunity to serve something much more important—he supplied Luke Skywalker with his lightsaber.

SNARE SLICER: Caught in an Ewok net with his rebel friends, R2-D2 sawed through the ropes and released them. Unfortunately, his actions did not save them from being tied up on poles to be roasted over an Ewok fire!

ASTROMECH ANTICS

R2-D2's singular moments extend well beyond his time in the socket of a starfighter.

FUNNY FELLOW

Even in the darkest hour, R2-D2 always finds a way to lighten the mood.

WITTY WARBLER: R2-D2 manages to express his intentions with just hoots and whistles. Yet those who understand his binary droidspeak are often amused and astonished at R2's devious sense of humor. The little droid can cut someone down to size in a few beeps.

DISTRACTION DROID: When General Grievous captured Anakin, Obi-Wan, and Chancellor Palpatine aboard his flagship, R2-D2 drew attention to himself by putting on an incredible sound-and-light display. This diversion gave Obi-Wan the chance to summon his lightsaber from Grievous and free himself and Anakin from their bonds.

EWOK ELECTRIFIER: Being tied to a roasting spit by Ewoks does not make for a happy droid. Once released, R2-D2 showed his gratitude by zapping the furry natives with his power probe.

MISHAP MACHINE

Though he delights in pointing out C-3PO's embarrassments, R2-D2 is not without some of his own.

JAWA JITTER: The Jundland Wastes on Tatooine are not a safe place for a solitary astromech unit rolling along on a secret mission. One shot of a stun gun caused R2 to shake and fall forward on his radar eye, making him easy pickings for Jawa scavengers.

BOG BELCH: When the murky swamps of Dagobah proved deeper than R2-D2's height, the droid raised his periscope eye above water level. What he didn't see was the beast swimming behind him with an open mouth. Fortunately, metal robots don't serve as a tasty meal, and the creature spat R2-D2 toward dry land.

R-SERIES

R2-D2 hails from a very successful line of R-series astromech droids designed and manufactured by Industrial Automaton. His galactic journeys have crisscrossed with many of his mechanical cousins, some of whom bear his likeness with subtle differences.

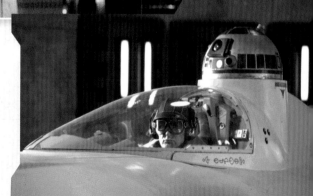

ROYAL NABOO SECURITY FORCES

Naboo's security chiefs invested heavily in acquiring a large quantity of cutting-edge astrodroids for their N-1 starfighters.

R2-A6 – Assigned to *Bravo 1*'s Ric Olié, the personal pilot for Queen Amidala and commander of the Naboo Royal Space Fighter Corps.

R2-C4 – Had panels the color of straw and was often socketed in *Bravo 6*.

QUEEN AMIDALA'S PERSONAL RETINUE

These droids had the distinction of serving aboard the queen's Royal Naboo Starship. Along with R2-D2, they braved fire from the Trade Federation to venture out onto the hull and make repairs. Sadly, only R2-D2 survived.

R2-M5 – Had a paint scheme similar to R2-D2 but with maroon trim.

R2-B1 – Boasted bright yellow panels and a royal blue body.

R2-R9 – Featured both a red body and trim.

G8-R3 – Possessed the main body unit of an R2-series droid topped by a flattop head.

20

INDEPENDENT OPERATORS

A few astrodroids have lost their owners and are left to find their own way in the galaxy.

R3-T7 – A malfunctioning, blast-scorched yellow-and-green-paneled astromech who roams the upper levels of Coruscant, forever searching for his master.

R2-A5 – A green-and-white unit last seen trundling the streets of Mos Eisley on Tatooine.

R3-T2 – Also a resident of Mos Eisley, bearing a red dome and a white body.

JEDI DROID POOL

The Jedi maintained their own contingent of astro-mechs primed for communal use.

R4-P17 – This red-domed unit often accompanied Obi-Wan Kenobi on missions during the Clone Wars. She tracked Jango Fett's *Slave I* to Geonosis and fought with Kenobi during the Battle of Coruscant, where buzz droids brought her to an unfortunate end.

R4-G9 – Trimmed in bronze, R4-G9 also saw action with Obi-Wan Kenobi during the Clone Wars. She piloted Kenobi's Eta-2 fighter away from Utapau so that Kenobi's presence on the planet remained unknown while he hunted for General Grievous.

R4-P44 – Flew an ARC-170 starfighter as part of Obi-Wan Kenobi's clone trooper detachment.

REBEL ROBOTS

The R2-series' quirky personality seems to lend these units naturally to freedom fighters.

R2-X2 – A white-and-green striped unit on the X-wing *Red 10* who was destroyed during the Battle of Yavin.

R3-A2 – An orange-paneled, clear-domed droid who was posted to the rebel base on Hoth.

R3-Y2 – A Hoth command center droid who helped the rebels evacuate from the ice world.

INQUISITIVE IMPERIALS

The Galactic Empire has thousands of R2 astromechs in its service. Often they are painted in a stark black-and-white scheme.

R2-Q2 – A member of the boarding party that captured the Alderaanian cruiser *Tantive IV*.

R3-T6 – Clear-domed with red trim, this droid had astronavigational duties on the first Death Star.

R2-Q5 – Stationed on the second Death Star, R2-Q5 had a polished black body and bronze paneling.

BEHIND THE SCENES

> "Artoo is the unsung hero of the two trilogies.
> He's the only one who knows the whole story."
> —*Star Wars* creator George Lucas

FASCINATING FIRSTS

❯ One movie myth long bandied about was that the name "R2-D2" originated from the shorthand heading on a "Reel 2, Dialogue 2" editing cue sheet for Lucas's earlier film, *THX 1138*. In actuality, Lucas invented the name because he liked its phonetic pronunciation.

❯ Concept artist Ralph McQuarrie designed the look of R2 from Lucas's own notes, adding multiple retractable arms as if the cylindrical repair droid was a robotic Swiss Army knife!

BEEPING 'BOT

❯ The noises babies make inspired sound designer Ben Burtt to create R2-D2's vocal palette. He recorded himself making the sounds and then electronically processed them for playback on a synthesizer.

❯ In early drafts of the *Star Wars* screenplay, R2-D2 didn't beep in binary at all but had actual dialogue!

INSIDE THE CAN

❯ For the original *Star Wars* film, production designer John Barry designed R2's body so the actor Kenny Baker could fit inside. Baker would rotate the dome and bounce the body, animating the droid as if it were alive.

❯ Though radio-controlled R2 units were used in the original trilogy, advancements in technology later permitted greater mobility and expressiveness. By the time *Revenge of the Sith* was made, a human no longer manipulated the robot internally. R2-D2 was either remotely controlled by droid builder Don Bies or created using computer-generated imagery.

TOP LEFT: Kenny Baker enjoys a moment of Tunisian sun on the *Star Wars* shoot as his R2 unit is fixed for the cameras. LEFT: A crew member presents the R2 chassis to actor Kenny Baker.

TOP: Ralph McQuarrie's original concept painting featuring the droids with a sleek, *Metropolis*-inspired look.
ABOVE: A preproduction design sketch by Ralph McQuarrie shows R2's inner workings.

ABOVE: The *Star Wars* production team assists R2-D2 operator Kenny Baker and C-3PO actor Anthony Daniels during a key scene from *Empire Strikes Back*.

BELOW: Joe Johnston created this early concept illustration showing the droids after being jettisoned from Jabba the Hutt's sail barge in *Return of the Jedi*.

ABOVE: A proud Kenny Baker watches R2-D2 roll off on his own on the set of *The Phantom Menace*.

ABOVE: A young George Lucas with an early R2-D2 prototype.

INTERVIEW WITH A DROID WRANGLER

DON BIES, A FORMER SPECIAL EFFECTS ENGINEER AT INDUSTRIAL LIGHT AND MAGIC (ILM), SERVED AS THE DROID UNIT SUPERVISOR ON THE *STAR WARS* PREQUELS. HE SHARES HIS EXPERIENCES FOR FELLOW R2 MODEL MAKERS.

HOW DID YOU FIRST BECOME INVOLVED WITH R2-D2?

When the original film came out, I built my own R2-D2—full-size and remote-controlled. Fast forward ten years, and I had moved to Northern California and was working in the film industry. I crossed paths with David Schaeffer, who Lucasfilm hired to operate one of the original radio-controlled R2s for personal appearances. David left to work at Disney as an Imagineer, so his droid position was open. I talked to those in charge, and R2 and I began working together. Our first job was a campaign for Panasonic in Japan.

HOW DID THIS LEAD TO BECOMING THE MAIN "PUPPETEER" FOR R2-D2 IN EPISODE I?

When they began production on *The Phantom Menace*, they shipped all the R2s (there were about sixteen) to the UK for filming. They began having some issues with things like controlling him on sandy surfaces. Since I had a twelve-year history with R2 (along with two colleagues I brought in to help, Nelson Hall and Grant Imahara), producer Rick McCallum called me from England one day to discuss the challenges they were facing. It was decided at that meeting that we would put together a team at ILM to create a new R2 unit that could overcome some of the issues. We created an R2 with a much stronger drive system and a little camera to operate it remotely. Once finished, I accompanied it to the UK for filming and spent six weeks on set. When I returned, I operated R2 for added shots at ILM. When *Attack of the Clones* rolled around, filming was moved to Sydney, Australia, and Rick asked me to head up the crew.

HOW DID YOU "ACT" VIA REMOTE CONTROL?

The movements of the radio-controlled R2 are very basic, so there was not much of a challenge "acting." If he was to be excited in a scene, I'd just make him more jumpy by rattling the joystick more—it wasn't the same caliber as Alec Guinness's acting!

CAN YOU DESCRIBE HOW THE TECHNOLOGY ADVANCED FROM THE ORIGINAL TRILOGY INTO AND THROUGH THE PREQUELS?

Essentially, we tried to make everything simpler—I felt that the simpler things were, the less there would be to repair if it broke down. We upgraded all the electronics but used the same motors that were installed from the days of *The Empire Strikes Back*. We created a quick change battery pack system so that the batteries could be replaced in about thirty seconds. Overall, the units were much more reliable, but that was mainly due to the advances in remote control technology.

WHY WAS R2'S PAINT SCHEME DIFFICULT TO REPLICATE FROM THE ORIGINAL TRILOGY? WHAT TIPS MIGHT YOU GIVE INCREDIBUILDS MODEL MAKERS?

For the original film, the creators used a type of semi-transparent blue paint that allowed the surface underneath to come through. Because of that style of paint, it was very difficult to nail down the color of blue—it would look very different in various types of light. For *The Phantom Menace*, the UK artists simply painted it

a flat blue. I wanted to bring the original color back as close as possible because I felt it really added to the character. It took a lot of experimentation to come up with a recipe that was close.

For those trying to replicate it, it's best to build up layers with a transparent royal blue over a shiny chrome or aluminum base. There are two stage paints commercially available that would get very close to the color.

SINCE YOU'VE SPENT SO MUCH TIME WITH R2 AND C-3PO, WHAT DO YOU THINK MAKES THEM TICK? WHY HAVE THEY MADE SUCH AN INDELIBLE MARK IN POPULAR CULTURE?

It's been said so many times, but they are archetypes. They provide comic relief, but they are actually well-drawn characters and really serve a purpose in the story, especially in the original films. And I also believe it's a great testament to the performers from the first films—Anthony Daniels really brings C-3PO to life, and the combination of effects techniques creates R2's character. Kenny Baker adds a human element to his subtle movements, and Ben Burtt's sound design creates R2's soul. All together, they have made for memorable characters.

MAKE IT YOUR OWN

One of the great things about IncrediBuilds models is that each one is completely customizable. The untreated natural wood can be decorated with paints, pencils, pens, beads, sequins—the list goes on and on!

Before you start building and decorating your model, though, read through the included instruction sheet so you understand how all the pieces come together. Then, choose a theme and make a plan. Do you want to make an exact replica of R2-D2 or something completely wacky? The choice is yours! Here are some examples to get those creative juices flowing.

It's a lot easier to craft R2-D2 *while* you build him. For all of the following projects, it is recommended to decorate the pieces with engraving on them *before* assembling the model.

R2-D2 REPLICA

When making a replica, it's always good to study an actual image of what you are trying to copy. Look closely at details and brainstorm how you can re-create them. R2-D2 is a very detailed model, so take your time and be patient.

WHAT YOU'LL NEED:
- Blue, silver, white, and red paint
- Small paintbrush

OPTIONAL:
- Detail paintbrush (such as a 18/0 spotter)
- Small, flat bright brush (recommended 1/8")
- Painter's or model tape

1. Start painting the engraved pieces with everything that should be white. Edge around details carefully. Let dry.

2. Paint in the silver where you want it to go. Let dry.

3. Paint in the blue where you want it to go, and add a final dab of red on R2-D2's front light.

4. After the engraved pieces are dry, assemble the model.

5. Finally, you can paint whatever is left— mainly R2-D2's legs and edges.

TIP: It's helpful to use colors in order from light to dark.

TIP: If you're having trouble making the lines straight, use a piece of painter's tape as a stencil. Simply tape around the area you want, and then paint inside. Wait until the paint is dry, and then lift up the tape. Voila!

MAKE IT YOUR OWN

R2-D2 IN THE SWAMPS OF DAGOBAH

You can also try re-creating R2-D2 in a specific scene from the *Star Wars* films. Here is R2-D2 as he emerges from the swamps of Dagobah on his mission to find Yoda with Luke Skywalker.

WHAT YOU'LL NEED:

- White, blue, and red colored pencils
- White, dark green, and brown paint
- Silver marker
- Paintbrush

OPTIONAL:

- An old dry paintbrush with rough bristles

For this model, you need to start with the R2-D2 Replica (page 29). A mixture of colored pencils and paint were used. (Colored pencils can make it easier to color in the details of the model.)

1. Follow steps 1 to 3 of the R2-D2 Replica. Replace paint with colored pencils and markers, but follow the same order of colors.

2. You can do one of two things next: Color the rest of the pieces with colored pencils, or assemble the model and use white paint to finish the edges and R2-D2's legs. White paint was used for this example.

3. Dab green and brown paint over the bottom half of the model. Don't be afraid to experiment! Use an old dry paintbrush with just a little paint for a speckled look. Press harder for more "blobs of mud." Layer the colors on top of each other. You can even blend some of the paint with your finger.

4. The top half of R2-D2 should be less swampy but still dirty. You'll want to carefully use your brush to drag some of the paint onto R2's top half. Sparser speckles work better than blobs here. You may even want to blend your brown paint with a little white to achieve a lighter effect.

5. Take your paintbrush and carefully dab more brown paint onto R2-D2's head. You don't want to overdo it, so be sparing.

Once you've achieved the look you want, you are finished! R2-D2 now looks just like he got pulled from the swamps of Dagobah!

R2-Q5

You can also turn R2-D2 into a whole other droid. This R2 unit worked for the Galactic Empire, serving aboard the second Death Star.

WHAT YOU NEED:
- Black, bronze, and silver paint
- Clear nail polish
- Tiny paint brush

OPTIONAL:
- Detail paintbrush (such as a 18/0 spotter)
- Small, flat bright brush (recommended 1/8")
- Painter's or model tape

1. Paint in the silver where you want it to go.
2. Paint in the bronze where you want it to go.
3. Let both silver and bronze paints dry.
4. Paint in the black, being careful to edge around the silver and bronze details.
5. Once the engraved pieces are dry, assemble the model.
6. Paint the unfinished pieces of the model black.
7. Once the paint is dry, add bronze stripes to the front of each leg,
8. Finally, to get a glossy finish, paint the entire model with clear nail polish. Make sure to have an adult help you with this part.

TIP: Since the main color of this model is black, the order of colors may seem backward. But it's important to follow the rule of lightest color to darkest. Again, paint all of the engraved pieces before assembling.

R4-P17

There are plenty of droids in the galaxy that you can turn your model into. This astromech unit worked for Obi-Wan Kenobi and served him well through many battles.

WHAT YOU NEED:
- White, black, dark red, and silver paint
- Tiny paint brush

OPTIONAL:
- Detail paintbrush (such as a 18/0 spotter)
- Small, flat bright brush (recommended 1/8")
- Painter's or model tape

This model is very similar to the R2-D2 Replica project from page 29. Please refer to those instructions for this.

Remember, it's important to paint from lightest color to darkest. In this case, the order will be:

1) White, **2)** Silver, **3)** Red, **4)** Black

The last thing to add is a color for R4's front light. It changes colors frequently in the films, so you can decide what you want. A light blue was used in this example.

SOURCES

Bouzereau, Laurent. *Star Wars: The Annotated Screenplays.*
New York: Del Rey, 1997.

Bray, Adam, Cole Horton, Kerrie Dougherty, and Michael Kogge.
Star Wars: Absolutely Everything You Need to Know.
New York: Dorling Kindersley, 2015.

Fry, Jason. *Star Wars: The Phantom Menace – The Expanded Visual
Dictionary.* New York: Dorling Kindersley, 2012.

Hidalgo, Pablo. "The History of R-Series Astromech Droids."
Star Wars Adventure Journal Vol. 7. August 1995. Honesdale,
PA: West End Games. 129-143.

Johnson, Shane. *Star Wars: Technical Journal* Vol. 1. Starlog
Magazine Presents, 1993.

Peterson, Lorne. *Sculpting a Galaxy.* San Rafael, CA:
Insight Editions, 2006.

Reynolds, David West, James Luceno, and Ryder Windham.
The Complete Star Wars Visual Dictionary. New York:
Dorling Kindersley, 2006.

Rinzler, J.W. *Star Wars: The Blueprints.* Seattle, WA: 47North, 2013.

———. *The Making of Star Wars: The Definitive Story Behind the Film.*
New York: Del Rey, 2007.

———. *The Making of Star Wars: Revenge of the Sith.* New York:
Del Rey, 2005.

Wallace, Daniel. *The Essential Guide to Droids.* New York:
Del Rey, 1999.

———. *The New Essential Guide to Droids.* New York: Del Rey, 2006.

Insight Editions would like to thank Curt Baker, Leland Chee,
Pablo Hidalgo, Samantha Holland, Daniel Saeva, and Krista Wong.

ABOUT THE AUTHOR

MICHAEL KOGGE'S other recent work includes *Empire of the
Wolf*, an epic graphic novel featuring werewolves in ancient Rome,
and the Star Wars Rebels series of books. He resides online at www.
MichaelKogge.com, while his real home is in Los Angeles.

IncrediBuilds™
A Division of Insight Editions LP
PO Box 3088
San Rafael, CA 94912
www.insighteditions.com

Find us on Facebook: www.facebook.com/InsightEditions
Follow us on Twitter: @insighteditions

Library of Congress Cataloging-in-Publication Data available.

ISBN: 978-1-68298-003-3

Publisher: Raoul Goff
Art Director: Chrissy Kwasnik
Designer: Jon Glick and Ashley Quackenbush
Executive Editor: Vanessa Lopez
Senior Editor: Chris Prince
Production Editor: Elaine Ou
Editorial Assistant: Katie DeSandro
Production Manager: Anna Wan
Production Coordinator: Sam Taylor
Craft and Instruction Development: Rebekah Piatte
Craft Photography: Anthony Piatte
Model Designer: Jianzhu He, Team Green

ROOTS of PEACE   REPLANTED PAPER

Insight Editions, in association with Roots of Peace, will plant two trees
for each tree used in the manufacturing of this book. Roots of Peace is an
internationally renowned humanitarian organization dedicated to eradicating
land mines worldwide and converting war-torn lands into productive farms and
wildlife habitats. Roots of Peace will plant two million fruit and nut trees in
Afghanistan and provide farmers there with the skills and support necessary
for sustainable land use.

Manufactured in China by Insight Editions

10 9 8 7 6 5 4 3